U0000209

A SLOTH'S GUIDE TO MINDFULNESS

樹懶的逆襲

BY TON MAK

鄭煥昇——譯

CHRONICLE BOOKS

SAN FRANCISCO

這本書獻給我的母親奧德莉，
是她在我還只有芝麻綠豆點大時，
就領著我進行第一次的靜坐體驗。

樹懶有時候真不好當。

Sometimes it's hard being a sloth.

生活也沒什麼進展。

Life feels a bit slow.

還必須費好大勁才能完成一些小事。

It takes a big effort to get small things done.

甚至連起床都是件不可能的任務。

Getting out of bed seems impossible.

工作像個無底洞。

Work seems endless.

有些日子，我們的心思跟火箭一樣快。

Our thoughts race at rocket speed.

想放慢腳步感覺超難。

Slowing down is hard.

想把每件事都做好更是難上加難。

But trying to do everything is even harder.

有些日子，我們會被惱人的小事弄得心神不寧。

Some days, everything is annoying.

嗨。

我們忘了種種幸福的小事。

但那些幸福的小事，早已存在我們身邊和心中。

We forget the small happy things.

Happy things that are already within us and around us.

操持正念，當下的幸福就會浮現。

Practicing mindfulness reveals the happiness in the present.

秉持正念，可以讓我們更加意識到周遭的美好。

Being mindful brings awareness of the wonders around us.

把心靈清空，好讓我們更明晰地看見當下。

We can see more clearly in the present by emptying our minds.

正念，不受時間的限制。

Mindfulness has no time restrictions.

它散落在各種日常的體驗裡。

It spreads through all mundane experiences.

樹懶
時報

追尋正念，沒有所謂的成功。

有些日子裡，你可能會找得有點辛苦。

但訣竅在於不要努力過頭。

The search for mindfulness is not marked by success.

Some days will be harder than others.

The key is not to try too hard.

對結果太執著，只會讓人更難活在當下。

If we focus too hard on results,

it becomes harder to stay present.

正念之王

✕

別這麼想。

活在當下，我們便能去觀察自己的
恐懼、憤怒、疑惑，
並更加意識到這些情緒。
Being in the moment, we can identify
our fear, anger, and doubt, and become
more aware of these feelings.

面對這些情緒你無須逃，也不必躲。

There is no need to run or hide from them.

跟你的情緒做朋友；好的壞的都不放過。

Befriend your emotions—the good ones and the bad ones.

負面情緒總是來來去去。

靜靜等它們過去就好。

Negative feels come and go.

It's OK to wait them out.

Relax.   放鬆。

Watch.   遠眺。

Reflect.   反思。

撐在那邊。

Hang in there.

暫停五分鐘，有時候就是最好的練習。

Sometimes just taking pause for five minutes
is the best practice.

淨空你的心靈，就像讓氣球洩氣一樣。

Empty your mind, like a deflating balloon.

壓力

妄念

想像把所有的壓力與負面思緒通通洗乾淨。

Visualize washing away all your stresses
and negative thoughts.

嗚……噓。

WOOOOOOSH.

想像你棲息在舒服的枝幹上。

Visualize resting on a snug branch.

又輕盈又放鬆。

Light and relaxed.

要是腦袋瓜依舊停不下來……

If your mind is still racing . . .

不要放棄。

don't give up.

咘嗚。

去陽光下散個步。

Take a walk in the sun.

給大自然一個大大的擁抱。

Give nature a big fat hug.

一笑置之。

Laugh it off.

呵、
呵、
呵。

在小地方表現善意。

Show small acts of kindness.

我發現了這個核桃，

然後就想起你的臉。

心存感激。

Be thankful.

有意識地活著，我們的幸福就會擴大。

When we live consciously our happiness expands.

吃飯，要細嚼慢嚥。

一口一口享受。

When eating, eat slowly.

Enjoy every bite.

與人說話時，要記得停下來傾聽。

When talking, pause to listen intently to others.

走路，

　　要用心去感受。

When walking,

　　walk mindfully.

別急。

No rush.

專注在當下。

Focus on the present moment.

沒能一直有所產出，不用擔心。

暫停一下沒關係。

It's OK to not be productive all the time.

It's OK to pause.

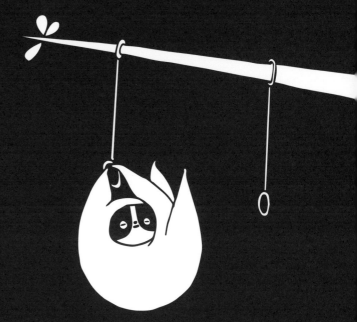

靜坐。

Meditate.

盤腿坐著，是個不錯的開始。

但說真的，你覺得舒服就行。

Sitting cross-legged is a good starting point.

But really, do what feels right.

捲成一團。

Curl up into a nugget.

直直站著。

Stand straight.

躺平。

Lie down.

做你自己就好。

You do you.

找到你內心的平靜。

緩緩閉上眼睛。

沉浸在你的舒適圈。

Find peace by finding your center.

Gently close your eyes.

Settle into your comfort zone.

確認一下你現在的感覺。

有沒有哪裡痛？

Check in with how you are feeling.

Is there any pain?

呼吸的時候感覺怎麼樣？

How does your breath feel?

將意識帶進你的身體。

觀察你身體與地面進行的每一次接觸。

感受你呼吸的一吸一吐。

注意你腹部隨著每次呼吸一脹一落的感覺。

Bring awareness to your body.

Observe any contact your body is making
with the ground.

Notice the feeling of your breath coming
in and out.

Notice the feeling of your belly as it
expands and falls with each breath.

專注於你的呼吸。

Focus on deep breathing.

吸氣。

Inhale.

吐氣。

Exhale.

想像你的呼吸在體內運行。

Imagine your breath running through your body.

別皺著眉頭。要笑。

No frowning. Smile.

如果心情搖擺不定，就試著專注在：

　　　　　你周遭的靜謐、

　　　　　你所處的空間、四下環境，

　　　　　以及你的呼吸。

If your mind wanders, try focusing on:

　　　　　the silence around you

　　　　　your space and surroundings

　　　　　your breathing

感受自己的思緒，但不要鑽牛角尖。

Be aware of your thoughts, but do not dwell on them.

你可能會因為一道強烈的情緒或稍縱即逝的念頭而分心。

You might be distracted by an intense feeling.

這時就緩緩地把注意力導引回來，重新專注在你的體感與呼吸上。

Gently redirect your attention back to the
sensations of your body and your breath.

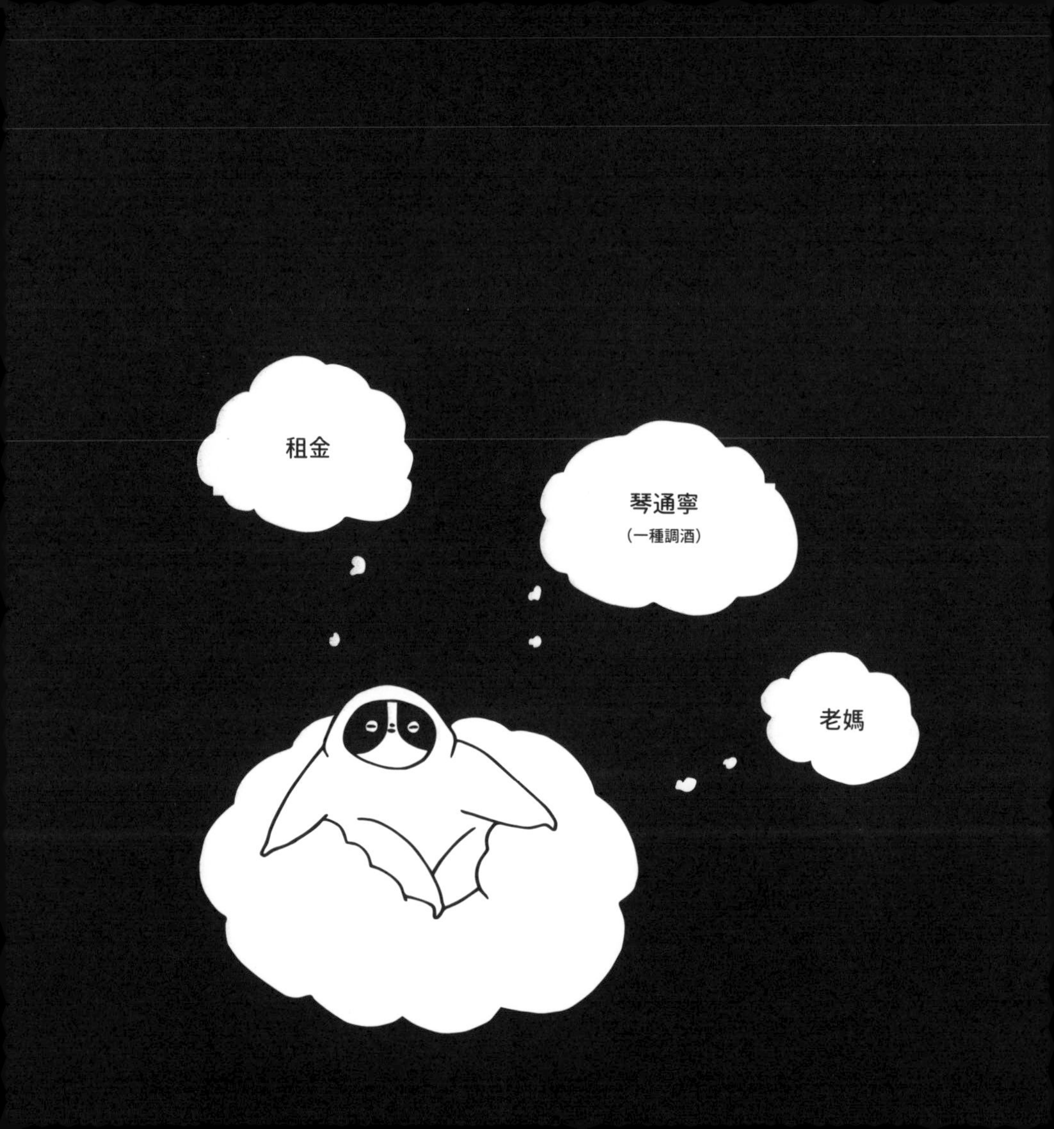
租金
琴通寧
（一種調酒）
老媽

你不可能讓所有的思緒都暫停，

所以不用去想該如何處理。

它們終究會自己過去。

It's impossible to stop all thoughts.

So leave everything as it is.

Eventually they will pass.

想要平靜地回到現實中時，就慢慢地睜開雙眼。

When you wish to return to the day, gently open your eyes.

慢慢地前進。

慢慢來，萬事OK。

Slowly move forward.

Slow is OK.

體會你身邊的美好。

Enjoy all the wonderful things around you.

最後的樹懶贈言……

Some final sloth words . . .

夢想可以大；
工作可以拚。
Dream big.
Work hard.

但別忘記要適時休息，

喝杯茶……

But remember to give yourself a break.

Drink some tea . . .

唱首歌……

sing a little . . .

在海上漂呀漂……

float in the ocean . . .

……或者找個舒服的地方坐著。

. . . or just sit someplace nice.

不用怕犯错。

Don't be afraid of making mistakes.

別有所保留，生命就會是一場精采的冒險。

Life can be an adventure if you don't hold yourself back.

吶，我這樣就好。

為自己站出來。

不需要趕路。

Stand up for yourself.

Go at your own pace.

傾聽你的內心。

Listen to your heart.

帶著信心往下跳。

Take a leap of faith.

面對眼前的風景，永遠心懷感激。

And always appreciate the current view.

特別感謝

━━━━━━━━━━━━━━━

一句大大的感謝獻給 Chronicle Books 的優秀團隊，謝謝他們對樹懶懷抱這麼多的愛與信賴：卡瑪仁・蘇布希雅、迪安・卡茲與艾莉森・維納。

謝謝我的家人、親朋好友，還有一路相挺我的工作室室貓班吉跟達斯提。

A big thank you to the wonderful team at Chronicle Books for having so much love and belief in the Sloth: Camaren Subhiyah, Deanne Katz, and Allison Weiner.

And thank you to my family, loved ones, and my supportive studio cats Benji and Dusty.

A SLOTH'S *GUIDE TO MINDFULNESS* by Ton Mak

Copyright © 2018 by FLABJACKS.

All rights reserved. No part of this book may be reproduced in any form without written permission from the publisher.

First published in English by Chronicle Books LLC, San Francisco, California.

This edition arranged with CHRONICLE BOOKS-CHILDREN

through Big Apple Agency, Inc., Labuan, Malaysia.

Complex Chinese edition copyright © 2019 China Times Publishing Company.

ISBN 978-957-13-7991-3

Printed in Taiwan.

Fun系列065

樹懶的逆襲：當競爭成為事實，耍廢就是義務！
A Sloth's Guide to Mindfulness

圖・文：Ton Mak｜譯者：鄭煥昇｜主編：陳家仁｜企劃編輯：李雅蓁｜美術設計：陳恩安｜企劃副理：陳秋雯｜第一編輯部總監：蘇清霖｜董事長：趙政岷｜出版者：時報文化出版企業股份有限公司／108019台北市和平西路三段240號4樓／發行專線：02-2306-6842／讀者服務專線：0800-231-705；02-2304-7103／讀者服務傳真：02-2304-6858／郵撥：19344724時報文化出版公司／信箱：10899臺北華江橋郵局第99信箱／時報悅讀網：www.readingtimes.com.tw｜法律顧問：理律法律事務所／陳長文律師、李念祖律師｜印刷：和楹印刷有限公司｜初版一刷：2019年11月22日｜初版五刷：2023年10月3日｜定價：新台幣350元｜版權所有　翻印必究（缺頁或破損的書，請寄回更換）

時報文化出版公司成立於一九七五年，並於一九九九年股票上櫃公開發行，
於二〇〇八年脫離中時集團非屬旺中，以「尊重智慧與創意的文化事業」為信念。

樹懶的逆襲：當競爭成為事實，耍廢就是義務！／Ton Mak 文、圖；鄭煥昇譯. -- 初版. -- 臺北市：時報文化，2019.11｜128面；15×15公分. --（Fun系列）；65｜譯自：A Sloth's guide to mindfulness｜ISBN 978-957-13-7991-3（平裝）｜1.人生哲學　191.9　108016791